# On Wings of Light

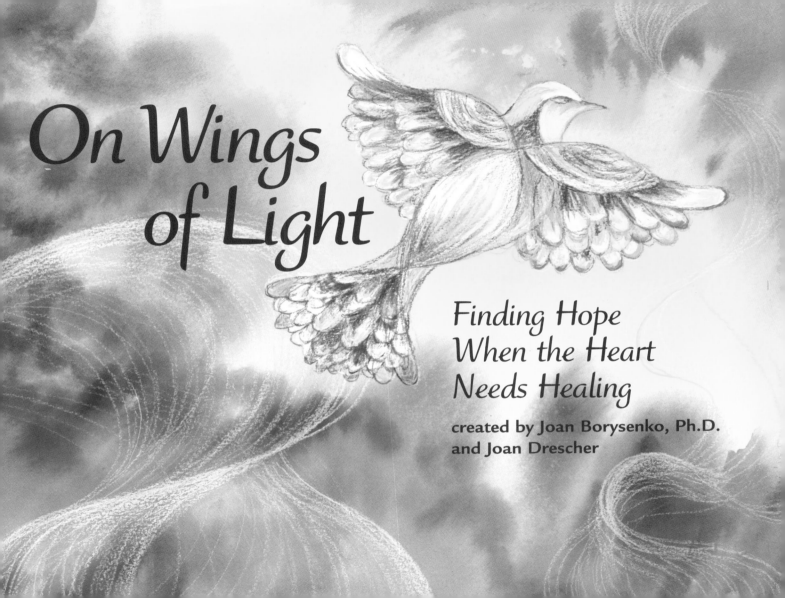

# On Wings of Light

## Finding Hope When the Heart Needs Healing

created by Joan Borysenko, Ph.D.
and Joan Drescher

The Institute for Body, Mind and Spirituality
Lesley University
29 Everett Street
Cambridge, MA 02138-2970

Printed in the United States of America
First printing: October 1992
First printing of revised edition: May 2003
10 9 8 7 6 5 4 3 2 1

Library of Congress Cataloging-In-Publication Data
Borysenko, Joan.
    On Wings of Light: Finding Hope When the Heart Needs Healing / co-created
    by Joan Borysenko and Joan Drescher.
        p.   cm.
     ISBN 0-9740377-0-2
     1. Inspiration.  2. Psychology.  3. Help   I. Drescher, Joan E.  II. Title
    BP605.N48B672003
    291.4'3–dc20                  2003105350
                                 CIP

Original Book Design by Giorgetta Bell McRee
Cover and Revised Design by Barbara Emmel Wolinsky, Trillium Studios, Norwell, MA
Back Cover Photo by Jean Abbott

# Dedication

To Elizabeth Lizer, Celia Thaxter Hubbard and Ken Drescher

# Acknowledgments

We are especially grateful to Tia and David Andrew, and David Moir, whose vision and generosity have made the republication of this book possible. The guiding spirit of Ron Moir is still present in all of us. He was the gardener who nourished the images of Joan Drescher's soul which blossomed and touched the lives of many. Ken Zeno, Director of The Institute for Body, Mind and Spirituality at Lesley University in Cambridge, MA, acted as midwife for the rebirth of this book under the auspices of Lesley University. His commitment included excellent feedback and the wonderful idea for the final section, *Reflections and Journaling*.

We wish to thank Barbara Wolinsky for her creative design expertise and dedication.

We have both been privileged to work with people who were suffering and ill, to witness their courage and be touched by their light. They are our teachers; we thank them all. We feel blessed to be working together again, sheltered by the wings of a long friendship and all the people who support us personally and in our work. You are too numerous to mention, but you know full well who you are.

## Introduction

This is a book about remembering
what we have always known in our hearts
but forgotten in our minds.


*That
Behind all appearances
Beyond the illusion of separateness
We are One
With ourselves, with each other and
With the Supernal Light of Creation*


*Bridges between Spirit and matter*


*We are the agents, the channels, the beings
Through which Love manifests in this world.
In this remembering lies our destiny,
Our hope, our joy and our healing.*

*On Wings of Light* was first published by Warner Books in 1992. Over the years we have received many letters from people who reconnected with hope, inspiration and courage by working with the book. We learned that the imagery, meditation and poetry worked together to create a felt experience of re-connection to the Divine. It kindled hope, not by words alone, but in some organic manner that touched the core of what it is to be human, living in an uncertain world, yet feeling safely held in the arms of a larger mystery.

Since 1992 the world has become ever more troubled. 911, an emergency call, has taken on an even more emergent meaning since the events of September 11, 2001. Economic uncertainty, terrorism and war, sickness and death—while always a part of the human condition—are more and more on our minds. The paradox of chaos and trouble is that it often contains within it the seeds of spiritual awakening and enlightened social action. In looking for our own courage, and healing the wounds of a broken heart, mind or body, we find that compassion and inner peace naturally grow. Our wounds become the mother of wisdom.

In our work with people who were suffering, we recognized the importance of inspiration. When you feel you are drowning, a life raft becomes the most precious gift in the world. We have been told that this book has served as a life raft for many. Then it went out of print. Then a small miracle occurred.

The Moir family, who had been a longtime supporter of Joan Drescher's (Joan D) art and healing work, offered to make the republishing of *On Wings of Light* possible. The reason you hold the second printing of the book in your hands is because they believed in it, and the necessity for a message and means of healing in this troubled time. Both Joan Borysenko (Joan B) and Joan D are affiliated with The Institute for Body, Mind and Spirituality at Lesley University in Cambridge, MA, and both are thrilled that Lesley University, in partnership with the Moir family, took on the job of re-publishing the book.

The seeds of *On Wings of Light* were planted when Joan B was an Instructor in Medicine at the Harvard Medical School and Director of a Mind/Body Clinic at one of Harvard's teaching hospitals. Her academic and personal fascination with the power of the mind to heal led to an exploration of imagination in healing. Images, of course, come from many sources: from our personal memories, from what Swiss psychiatrist C.G. Jung called the "collective unconscious" that is available to all and from what we see and experience in the world around us. Negative images create fear, which can also affect the body negatively. Hopeful images, in contrast, can bring forth the love and peace of mind that optimize physical health and support the process of healing. Studies indicate that hospitalized patients whose rooms have a view of nature (a healing image) mend faster and are released from the hospital sooner than patients whose rooms face a parking lot. These kinds of studies have prompted many hospitals to incorporate healing images through architecture, plantings, music and art.

Joan D has been creating murals in hospitals for the last 20 years and is a pioneer in bringing beauty to dark places. As artist-in-residence at Boston's MassGeneral Hospital for Children, she experiences daily how color and images can help her patients communicate from a deeper, truer place than words. Art serves as a bridge between patients and those who care for them. It also helps create a healing environment, decreasing pain and stress. Perhaps the most intriguing aspect of healing art is its capacity to reconnect us with our souls and to life as a sacred journey.

It is a convenience of expression to say that Joan B wrote the text and Joan D illustrated the book. Both the text and the images were presented to us from a Higher Source that we both tapped into concurrently. The original process of writing was full of delightful synchronicities—little miracles that let us know that the same Divine mind was working through us both. That you are reading it now is no coincidence. It is by Divine appointment that it has found its way to you.

The images on these pages are meant to bring forth your own images, to help you remember, to bring back home again the disparate parts of yourself lost to the pains and stresses of life. Home is the peaceful place inside you. It is where love, truth, wisdom, creativity and Spirit reside. Through the simple process of enjoying this book, and then reflecting on and journaling your experience in the last section, we hope to help you reconnect with soul and Spirit. It is our heartfelt intention that this book will help give you the courage to see even darkness as a blessing.

Through the images present here, and those evoked in your mind, we hope you will experience your own good heart, and the reality that behind all appearances, beyond the illusion of separateness, we are all One. As you heal so do your family, the people with whom you work, your community and ultimately the world.

This book is meant to help you have authentic inner experiences that will restore hope and the faith that your life is happening just as it should. By helping you see beauty and meaning in the dark places, the images in these pages can uplift you. But even more important, they can inspire you to pay attention to the healing images and symbols within and all around you.

Pictures of butterflies, symbols of transformation, were carved into barrack walls in Nazi death camps by the children. In the midst of intense suffering, the indwelling Spirit of Guidance spoke to these children through their imaginations, conveying through symbolism what words would have been powerless to express. Just as a caterpillar dies to give birth to a butterfly, so would the death of the children birth their magnificent souls. By carving this powerful image of immortal Spirit on the walls, the children were able to have hope and comfort in an apparently hopeless situation.

In her work with hospitalized children and adults, Joan D has found that color is an important part of how the imagination creates healing images. The process of experimenting with color and creating simple art can transform even a hospital environment into sacred space. Some patients experience such profound pain relief in the process, they actually require less medication. A child so traumatized that he could not speak finally found words after expressing himself through colorful symbols.

You might enjoy closing your eyes and relaxing into the inner imagery that the color, shapes and archetypal symbols evoke in this book. Symbols are a shorthand that your other-than-conscious mind immediately recognizes. Symbols can be profoundly strengthening and inspiring. Perhaps you will find special ones that you can carry with you in your mind or re-create by drawing or by clipping out similar symbols from books and magazines. These images can give you courage when you are scared, hope when you are despairing, and reconnection to the Divine source when you feel most isolated and alone.

The body-mind system has an innate inner wisdom that knows what we need for our healing. Although our deepest wisdom presents images and symbols to us constantly both in dreams and in waking life, we tend to be so engaged in conscious thought that we ignore these healing gifts. One purpose of this book is to help you focus your attention on the images that your other-than-conscious mind is always providing, and to create a strong intention to work with these images. Specific instructions for working with healing imagery are given in the section on *Reflections and Journaling* at the end of the book.

Once upon a time
love erupted with a mighty roar.
A ball of living, breathing light exploded into a universe
of fire and ice, suns and moons, plants and animals, you and me.
Since that first moment love has known itself
and expanded itself through us.
Our joys and sorrows, hopes and fears, our dissolution in night's soft womb
and re-creation in the morning's song are reflections of the divine love
that plays its infinite melodies on the tender strings of our hearts.
The notes of anguish, exultation and anger, delight, pain and grace
unite in a sacred harmony when we remember
that behind all appearances;
beyond the illusion of separateness
We are One.

In that remembering
we can rejoice in our divine birthright
as children of love's first light.
Come and let us remember together.

Take a deep breath and let your body relax...
feel yourself sinking into the arms of matter
all the while remembering your Divine Source.

I am a bridge between heaven and earth.
The love of creation flows through me.

Can you remember arriving from the far corners of the universe
and tucking your lightself into human form?

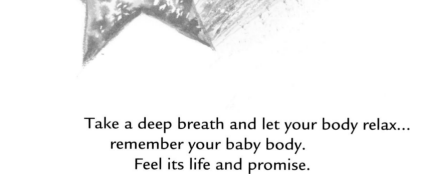

Take a deep breath and let your body relax...
remember your baby body.
Feel its life and promise.
Feel its peace and power.

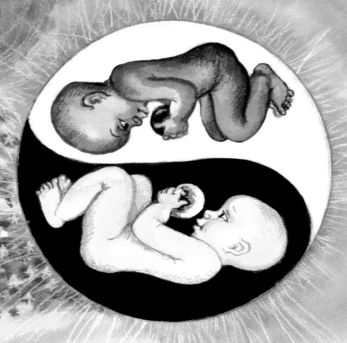

The full potential of the universe is present within me.

Can you remember what your favorite story was when you were in your child body?
Take your time and bring your awareness to each image.
Notice the way that your breath and body respond.

Take a deep breath and let your body relax...
feel the magic and mystery of the stories deep within.

I am a being of power, radiance and mystery.

Life is a creative adventure.

Can you remember when we sat by the fire and told
stories of the hunt, stories of the sky,
stories of the Great Mother who gives and nourishes life?

I am safe in the arms
of mother earth
and grandfather sky.

Can you remember...

Breathing the earth in through your feet and your nose and your eyes and feeling connected to all of nature?

Take a deep breath and let your body relax...
remember a time when your whole body
resonated with the pulse of the earth.

I am connected to all that is, at one with the wholeness of life.

Can you remember
when you fell asleep
to the radiance and memories
that you are?

When you forgot the stories
of our ancestors,
the lullabies of our mother,
the magic of our childhood?

When did you come to believe
in the lies of darkness,
the illusion that you are isolated,
unworthy, unlovable
or otherwise separate
from the Whole?

*It is time to wake up again*
*and remember who you really are.*

I can wake up now.
   I can remember who I really am.

I can feel life arising freshly within me, awakening my memories.
   Take a deep breath and feel the life-force in your body.

I am a child of the one light,
a bridge between heaven and earth.
When love flows across that bridge
miracles happen.

I can travel the universe
on wings of light
as long as I remember my connection
to the source of our being.

*I can remember by paying attention to my breath.*

Become aware of the flow of your breathing.
Breathe light in through the top of your head.
Breathe light out through the soles of your feet.

Sense the inner tides as your whole body
swells with the inbreath, lets go with the outbreath.

The ancient marriage of earth and sky, moon and sea
is consummated in the sacred rhythm of your breath.
Take time to be present to the flow.

Earth and sky, fire and water, spirit and matter unite in me.
My breath is one with the heartbeat of the universe.

*I can remember by reflecting on a time when I was completely present to life.*

A holy moment. A time when the mystery revealed itself to me in
the eyes of a child, or the light of the moon resting on the
breast of the sea. A time when a glimpse of starlight, the
colors of a rainbow or the face of my beloved became the whole of eternity.

Take a deep breath and let your body relax
think back to a time when you felt at one with nature, yourself, a pet or another person.
Go inside yourself, closing your eyes if you like.
Remember the sights...the sounds...the fragrances...the sensations.

The peace, love, gratitude and joy that these memories awaken
are your own true nature, your highest self. It is through that
self that we help bring the world into being. It is in that self
that we are most fully human and most completely divine.

The whole of eternity is present in each moment.
When I live my life one moment at a time, one breath at a time,
I live from my highest self which is one with all.

*I can remember by paying attention to what is*
*rather than living in the movies of my mind.*

Pretend that you are a stranger in a strange land.
Engage your full attention by focusing on your breathing...
now open your senses newly to the world around you.
Take several minutes to notice:

What do you see?
What do you hear?
What do you touch?
What do you feel?
What do you know in your heart?

Peace of mind is my own true nature.
I claim it by letting go of the past and future,
paying attention to what is.

*I can remember by embracing every activity as sacred.*

Sewing on a button,
working in the garden,
doing the wash,
driving down the freeway,
going to work.

To be present is to be joyful.
To be joyful is to radiate love.
To radiate love is to heal
and be healed.

I am present to all things, all circumstances
and all people without judgment.
I can see God in everything.

I can remember by taking responsibility when I act out of ignorance or fear, and then forgiving myself.

*I accept my errors as teachings in wisdom and compassion.*

*I can remember by expressing lovingkindness.*

Take a deep breath and relax your body as you exhale slowly.
Imagine that you are standing in a beam of sunlight.

Think of all the things you have experienced in this lifetime.
Joy and sorrow, wonder and sadness, love and loss, births and deaths.

Bring to mind the child you once were and with reverence,
respect and love for all that child has endured in its search for wisdom,
repeat these lovingkindness blessings for yourself.


*May I be at peace.*
*May my heart remain open.*
*May I remember the beauty of my own true nature.*
*May I express my fullest potential.*
*May I be healed.*

Imagine your loved ones, one by one, or in a group standing in the beam of sunlight.

*May you be at peace.*
*May your heart remain open.*
*May you remember the beauty of your own true nature.*
*May you be healed.*

Imagine any person or persons that you are in conflict with standing in the beam of sunlight.

*May you be at peace.*
*May your heart remain open.*
*May you remember the beauty of your own true nature.*
*May you be healed.*

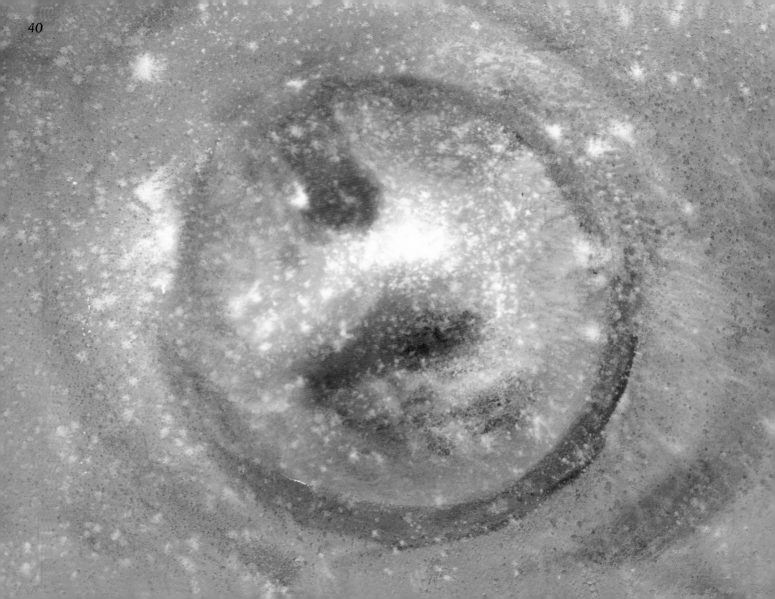

Imagine our beautiful earth,
hanging like a jewel in the starry vastness of space.

The blue seas, the green continents,
the white clouds.

A living, breathing being of
fire and water…earth and sky…
minerals and plants…
animals and human beings.

*May there be peace on earth.*     *May the hearts of all people be open to one another.*

*May all life reach its highest potential.*        *May all life reflect the glory of the light.*

*I can remember by believing*
*that whatever is happening,*
*no matter how strange, or sad or painful,*
*is happening in love's service.*

I am perfectly and eternally safe.

The radiance that tucked itself into my baby body and my child body,
the radiance of love, wisdom and creation is still present within me.

It was present before my body was and will be present
when my body is no more.
It is present in the fire, in the stories, in the ancestors and the stars.

It is present as who I am and evermore shall be.
The Great One who is ever reflecting life
back to itself as *itself.*

I am the soul of the world
and the Song of Songs.
My life is a wonder and a blessing.

I need only remember.

# Reflections and Journaling
## Using Imagery for Healing

**What you will need:**

• An open mind and an open heart. Remember yourself as a five-year-old filled with the excitement of creativity and self-discovery. Even if apparently negative images come up for you, honor them rather than judging or rejecting them. You can even have an imaginary conversation with the image and record the dialogue in your journal.

• A spiral-bound notebook, journal or sketchpad with unlined paper that opens up so that the pages lie flat. Look for thick paper of good quality.

• A special pen that feels good in your hand and flows easily. You might enjoy having several pens of different colors.

• Your choice of art materials. They could be as simple as a box of crayons or colored pencils, or perhaps you might prefer oil crayons or paints. The choices are endless. It can also be fun to create collages by cutting out images from magazines or using personal pictures.

• A sacred space in which to work. What this means is personal to you. It might be a picnic table under your favorite tree, or just a corner of a room indoors with your favorite music playing in the background. Sacred space is safe, a place apart from the busyness of daily life where you can be alone without interruptions. It is soul space.

**How to Begin:**

• Read through the entire book slowly, savoring the images and the way that your body responds to them. Which images capture your imagination? Different images speak to different people. Work with the ones that call out to you. For example, on pages 14 and 15, the images are from childhood stories. You are asked if you can remember your own favorite childhood story. Joan D remembers the adventures of Alice in Wonderland, delighting in the feeling that her body could be any size and that she could fit into small places. That is a powerful body memory that stimulates the recollection of her full potential as a human being.

Joan B recalls a story about a sick princess who could only be healed by receiving a piece of the moon. Her body memory of the story is a felt-sense of power, of life-force energy, and of comfort that comes both from the moon and from the love of the father who tries to get it for her. For both Joans, there is a strong body sense of power and healing in the stories they recalled.

The images, words, music or other sensory experiences that capture feelings of healing are powerful medicine. Images, in particular, can be food for the soul. You can quest for them, like the mythological Jason looking for the Golden Fleece. For Joan B, images of the moon have an almost magical healing power. They are like talismans. If you find such an image for yourself, recreate it on the cover of your journal. Make your journal a multimedia experience, using the full range of your creativity to express yourself in words, images or even simple splashes of color.

## Questions for Reflection and Journaling

Turn your book to the pages listed below for each exercise of reflection. Take a few minutes to savor the images and feelings they evoke. Become one with the images in your own way. Then reflect on the text and the questions asked about each image. Record your reflections in your multi-media journal.

### Images on Pages 10 - 11

*Feel yourself sinking into the arms of matter all the while remembering your Divine Source.*

Can you imagine yourself before you took birth and entered your body? Some people talk about a Divine Light of love and wisdom that they merge with during near-death experiences. Some people report seeing or feeling light in the room where a baby is born. Can you imagine yourself as part of that light? How does that light carry over into matter? What else can you imagine or remember?

### Images on Pages 12 - 13

*Remember your baby body. Feel its life and promise. Feel the full potential of the universe within you.*

What does potential feel like inside you? Do you think that you, or anyone, has a divine purpose, a specific calling? If you believe in the concept of life purpose, what do you think yours is? Does your life track with that purpose? Can you remember how some of your most difficult life experiences helped you realize your purpose and potential? Take time to reflect in writing and imagery about what you learned through life's challenges.

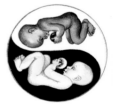

## Images on Pages 14 - 15

### *Can you remember what your favorite story was when you were in your child body?*

Write down your favorite story in your own words. What do you most relate to about it? How did it make you feel as a child? How does it make you feel right now? Are there any images in the story that feel especially powerful? What is the most important message in the story? How might it relate to the story of your own life right now? Are there any other stories that you need to remember to help you along your journey today?

## Images on Pages 16 - 17

### *I am a being of power, radiance and mystery. Life is a creative adventure.*

Children are born as curious, creative, spontaneous beings. Life is an adventure. As adults we often forget that. Can you remember the joy and wonder that you felt as a child, the feeling that all things were possible and that life was filled with magic? Record a childhood memory that captures that feeling. Can you still feel that promise of life's adventure unfolding? When do you feel most alive? Most creative? What could you do to make your life a creative adventure right now? For example, Joan B is taking tango lessons. Is there one small step you could take?

**Images on Pages 18 - 19**
*I am safe in the arms of mother earth and grandfather sky.*

What are the stories of Creation, of how the earth and her children came into being, that speak to you most deeply? Do these stories help you feel safe or not? Do they nourish you and bring out your potential, wisdom and compassion? Are your beliefs about God rooted in experience or are they simply concepts handed down from others? Try writing and illustrating your own Creation story.

**Images on Pages 20 - 21**
*Feeling connected to all of nature.*

Reflect on the last time that you felt connected to nature. How did that connection feel in your body? What were the sights, sounds, smells and emotions that you experienced? Is there a healing place in nature that you can visit in your life now? Is there a healing place that you can visit in your mind? Write about that place and create images of it in your journal, either through drawing, pasting in favorite photos or clipping out images from magazines. You might even collect leaves or flowers to press and include in your journal. The more specific your inner map of this sacred, healing place, the more powerful it will be as a mental sanctuary that you can visit any time.

**Image on Page 22**

*Can you remember when you fell asleep to the radiance and the memories that you are?*

Life challenges are both a danger and an opportunity. The danger is that you can lose hope and become depressed. The opportunity is that a whole new life can emerge. Write about a time when you experienced a dark night of the soul, when you forgot your creative potential and believed that you were isolated, unworthy or unlovable. What brought you out of the darkness into the light? Can you list three things that helped you heal? Can you capture the power of that healing in an image or a symbol?

**Image on Page 23**

*It is time to wake up again and remember who you really are.*

Healing images like the bird in the window can awaken you to the Spiritual Self that is your own true nature of wisdom, peace, compassion and power. Images of the Spiritual Self often appear during dark nights of the soul, and can become long-lasting symbols of hope and courage. Discovering and paying attention to these symbols can help you stay awake to who you really are. For example, an eagle came to Joan B during a difficult time. She placed pictures of eagles around her home and often wears a silver eagle pendant to remind her of the Spirit within. A powerful image of a hot air balloon came to Joan D during a time of darkness and transformation. That image became a book, *The Moon Balloon*, which has helped hundreds of children to heal and helped Joan fulfill an important part of her life's purpose.

# Waking Up to Who You Really Are

Symbols can help us wake up to the mystery of life and to who we really are. They can also help keep us awake so that the inevitable busyness and challenges of life have a harder time hiding the true light of our souls. This next part of the book consists of visual symbols, guided meditations and affirmations to help you stay awake to the light that you are.

### Images on Pages 24 - 25
***I am a child of the one light, a bridge between heaven and earth.***
***When love flows across that bridge, miracles happen.***

Open your journal, prepared to think in both words and images. Bring to mind a time when you felt love flowing through you. Where were you? How did it feel in your body? How did it feel in your heart? When was the last time you felt as though you were a child of the one light? Write down all the miracles you have experienced. Is there a common image or symbol that unites them?

### Images on Pages 26 - 27
***I can travel the universe on wings of light as long as I remember my connection***
***to the Source of our being.***

Close your eyes and settle down into your body and the rhythm of your breathing. Imagine that you are the bird, traveling through the universe on wings of light. Where do you go? What do you see? How do you feel? What do you remember? Journal this experience in both word and image.

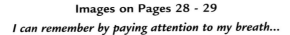

**Images on Pages 28 - 29**
*I can remember by paying attention to my breath...*

After experiencing the meditation on breath and light on page 32, use your journal to record your experiences in word and image. What is your connection to the Divine Source?

**Images on Pages 30 - 31**
*I can remember by reflecting on a time when I was completely present to life.*

After experiencing the meditation on a holy moment, a time when you were in the Now, journal about it. What did your body feel like? What sensations did you remember? What were the colors, feelings, scents, and images that came to mind? Is there a particular sensation that draws you back into that experience? Almost every spiritual tradition talks about Presence, the direct perception of things as they are, rather than our thoughts about things. Presence, being in the Now, is a taste of heaven. It has been described as total relaxation, spaciousness and peace. What does Presence feel like to you? How might you remind yourself to experience it more often in daily life? Is there a symbol that brings you back to Presence? Can you use your breath as a way to get there?

**Images on Pages 32 - 33**
*I can remember by paying attention to what is, rather than living in the movies of my mind.*

Take your journal out into nature. With beginner's mind—the mind of a stranger in a strange land who has never seen the earth before—find an object of beauty and let it speak to you. Hold it in your hand and look at it closely. Smell it, observe the way that light plays off of it. Can you become one with the object and see it with your soul? What do you notice? Follow the contour of the object with your eyes and record it spontaneously with your pencil or pen without worrying what the end result will be. Describe the object as your soul sees it: through the eyes of the heart.

**Images on Pages 34 - 35**
*I can remember by embracing every activity as sacred.*

Choose one activity today that you would normally take for granted. For example, taking a shower. When you do so, be as mindful and present as possible. Let go of your thoughts. Feel the sensations of the water and soap. This mundane moment is also a holy moment. Now is the only time there is. When you are finished, sit with your journal for a few moments. What did you notice? Can you express any of your feelings or perceptions in colors or symbols?

**Images on Pages 36 - 37**
*I can remember by taking responsibility when I act out of ignorance or fear, and then forgiving myself.*

Tonight before bed retrospect your day, beginning with the last thing that happened and working your way back toward morning. Notice the times when you were in the Now, awake and remembering your connection to life. Notice the times when you felt out of sorts, out of the Present, out of right relationship to your higher self. Were there times when you acted out of fear or ignorance? If so, think about how you might have acted differently. If there are amends to be made, vow to make them as soon as possible. If you do this exercise each night, regrets and resentments have no time to fester. You can sleep in peace, having created forgiveness by taking responsibility for your thoughts and actions, learning from them and vowing to act from your best self.

**Images on Pages 38 - 39**
*I can remember by expressing lovingkindness.*

The blessings of lovingkindness that you say for yourself (at the bottom of page 38) are also said for loved ones, enemies and all beings. All people want the same things—to be well and happy, to be open hearted, to be free from suffering and harm. It is a wonderful practice to repeat these blessings in the morning when you arise, at night before you go to sleep and anytime during the day that you want to pray for someone, send love or relieve conflict. Try sending the lovingkindness blessings with light and color as well as with words. Visualize the recipient, and imagine wrapping them in swirls of rainbow light, healing light. You can also draw a picture of the person in your journal and write the prayer next to their image. Writing the blessings of lovingkindness on a note card, which you can also illustrate, is a beautiful gift of spirit that you can send to people.

**Images on Pages 40 - 41**
*Imagine our beautiful earth hanging like a jewel in the starry vastness of space.*

Sending blessings of lovingkindness to our mother earth is particularly important in this time of environmental chaos and pollution. Meditate on the image of our planet rotating through the cosmos. Think of how precious the gift of life is—both for yourself and for the earth, which is a living being, just as you are. How can you bless the earth in a practical way? Is there one act that you can commit to that would make a difference, for example, joining a carpool or taking the bus to work even once per week. What is the one thing you can do to honor life on our small planet?

**Images on Pages 42 - 43**
*May there be peace on earth.*

The earth's people—black and red, white and yellow—are holding hands in peace and understanding. What does this mean to you in a practical way? How can you help bring this about in your own community? Even volunteering at a nursing home, a youth program, or a homeless shelter for a few hours a month makes a positive impact. Even though you are just one of almost five billion people in this world, you have the power to make a difference. Your actions affect your family, your community, your nation and all people. Peace on earth begins with peace in each person. War has never worked. It is time to give peace a chance.

We congratulate you for taking the time to water the seeds of your awakening, and to remember what an important part of this interdependent universe you are. We hope that this book will be a continuing source of comfort and inspiration that will help you remember your own true nature.

You can remember by believing
That whatever is happening
No matter how strange, or sad, or painful
Is happening in love's service.
You are perfectly and eternally safe.

The radiance that tucked itself into your baby body
And your child body,
The radiance of love, wisdom and creation
Is still present within you.

It was present before your body was
And will be present when your body is no more.
It is present in the fire, in the stories,
In the ancestors and the stars.

It is present as who you are and evermore shall be.
The Great One
Who is ever reflecting life
Back to itself as itself.

*Joan Borysenko* has been described as "a rare jewel: respected scientist, gifted therapist and unabashed mystic."* A powerful and articulate teacher and writer, Dr. Borysenko has a clear vision: to bring science, psychology and spirituality together in the service of health, happiness and inner peace. Joan completed both her doctoral and post-doctoral work at the Harvard Medical School in cancer cell biology and behavioral medicine. She is also a clinical psychologist and co-founder and former director of the mind-body clinical programs at the Beth Israel Deaconess Medical Center in Boston on which her New York Times bestseller, *Minding the Body, Mending the Mind* was based. President of Mind-Body Health Sciences, LLC, she is the author of eleven books on integrative medicine, psychology, spirituality, women's studies and inner peace, in addition to numerous meditation tapes, lecture programs and videos.

For more information on Joan's work, her company, a complete listing and description of books and tapes, or to order products, please go to her website. Her monthly newsletter, to which you are warmly invited to subscribe, is also archived on the website:

**www.joanborysenko.com**

or

**Mind-Body Health Sciences, LLC**

393 Dixon Road

Boulder, CO 80302

303-440-8460 tel

303-440-7580 fax

luziemas@aol.com

*\* Dean Ornish, M.D., president and director, the Preventative Medicine Research Institute, University of California, San Francisco*

*Joan Drescher's* pioneering work, using art to mend both body and spirit, has been recognized internationally. Her healing murals are to be found in major hospitals throughout the U.S. and Canada.

Joan is a writer and illustrator of more than 25 children's books, including *The Moon Balloon — A Journey of Hope and Discovery for Children and Families.* This book has helped families in the U.S. and Europe go through change, transition and loss.

She explores the vital connection between medicine, art and the healing process in her inspiring visual presentations. Joan is the Artist-In-Residence at MassGeneral Hospital for Children in Boston where she invites young patients to create their own visual journals and regularly offers workshops and training in the arts to doctors, residents and other healthcare professionals. She is also a Fellow of The Institute for Body, Mind and Spirituality at Lesley University.

For more information on Joan's work, custom murals and workshops, as well as to order books and fine art prints of original watercolor illustrations from *On Wings Of Light,* please visit her website at:

**www.themoonballoon.com**
or
**Murals for Healing Environments**
23 Cedar Street
Hingham, MA 02043
781-749-5179 tel
balloon@world.std.com

*The Institute for Body, Mind and Spirituality* at Lesley University was established for the purpose of promoting inquiry, training professionals, conducting research, developing new programs and providing leadership in the area of mind-body health and education. Health is broadly defined as a dynamic process of well-being, which integrates mental, physical, social/relational, aesthetic and spiritual elements. The fostering of this process relies upon primary prevention efforts, in addition to the treatment of disease. Drawing upon our expertise in the areas of counseling psychology, creative arts, expressive therapies, education, interdisciplinary studies and management, the Institute is committed to the integration of holistic principles and methods into professional practice within a diverse society. The Institute adheres to a transformational approach to education and to the application of the principles of reflective practice. IBMS incorporates Lesley University's mission of empowering students and professionals with the knowledge, skills and experience to succeed as leaders and catalysts in their professions and within their communities

The Institute for Body, Mind and Spirituality offers training in Professional Continuing Education in the fields of education, mental and physical health for licensed mental health counselors, pastoral counselors, expressive therapists, psychotherapists, social workers, somatic and complementary health practitioners, teachers and school counselors and arts specialists. The goal of these workshops is to provide innovative educational opportunities, which will expand the boundaries of professional knowledge, promote dialogue about and advance the investigation and integration of body-mind-spirit theory and methods in professional practice. Workshops are also open to the public.

The Institute also produces occasional monographs in the field of Mind-Body-Spirit and conducts research in related disciplines. For more information:

**THE INSTITUTE FOR BODY, MIND AND SPIRITUALITY at LESLEY UNIVERSITY**

29 Everett St., Cambridge, MA 02138-2970

contact Ken Zeno at 617-349-8179 or 800-999-1959 ext. 8179

or go to www. lesley.edu/gsass/bodymind

LESLEY
UNIVERSITY